EVERYDAY RELIGION

My Christian Life

Alison Seaman

WAYLAND

EVERYDAY RELIGION

My Buddhist Life
My Christian Life
My Hindu Life
My Jewish Life
My Muslim Life
My Sikh Life

Editor: Ruth Raudsepp
Designer: Joyce Chester

First published in 1996 by Wayland Publishers Ltd, 61 Western Road, Hove, East Sussex, BN3 1JD, England.

© Copyright 1996 Wayland Publishers Ltd

British Library Cataloguing in Publication Data
Seaman, Alison
My Christian Life – (Everyday Religion)
1. Christianity – Juvenile literature
2. Christians – Juvenile literature
I. Title
248

ISBN 0 7502 1298 5

Picture acknowledgements
The author and publishers thank the following for taking photographs and for giving permission to reproduce photographs: David Rose 7, 8, 9, 12, 14, 20, 21, 25, 26; Alison Seaman 15; Zak Waters 10, 16; Barry Webb 6; Andes Press Agency 13; Chris Fairclough 5; Ffotograff/Charles Aithie 18; Topham Picture Point 8; Travel Ink/David Toase 24.
The remaining pictures are from the Wayland Picture Library.

Typeset by Joyce Chester
Printed in Italy by G. Canale S.p.A.

Contents

The Bible 5
Christmas 6–7
Going to Church 8–9
Sunday School 10–11
Baptism 12–13
Confirmation 14–15
Prayer 16–17
Worship 18–19
Palm Sunday 20
A Special Meal 21
Easter 22–23
A Christian Wedding 24
Remembrance 25
Jesus 26
A Christian Prayer 27
Notes for Teachers 28–29
Glossary 30
Further Information 31
Index 32

These children are all **Christians**. There are Christians all over the world. It is like being part of one big family.

Anna is reading one of her favourite stories from the **Bible**. It is about a special person called **Jesus**.

Christmas is the time when Christians celebrate the birth of Jesus. Stuart and Emily are giving their grandpa a present.

Christians believe that Jesus was a very special gift from God.

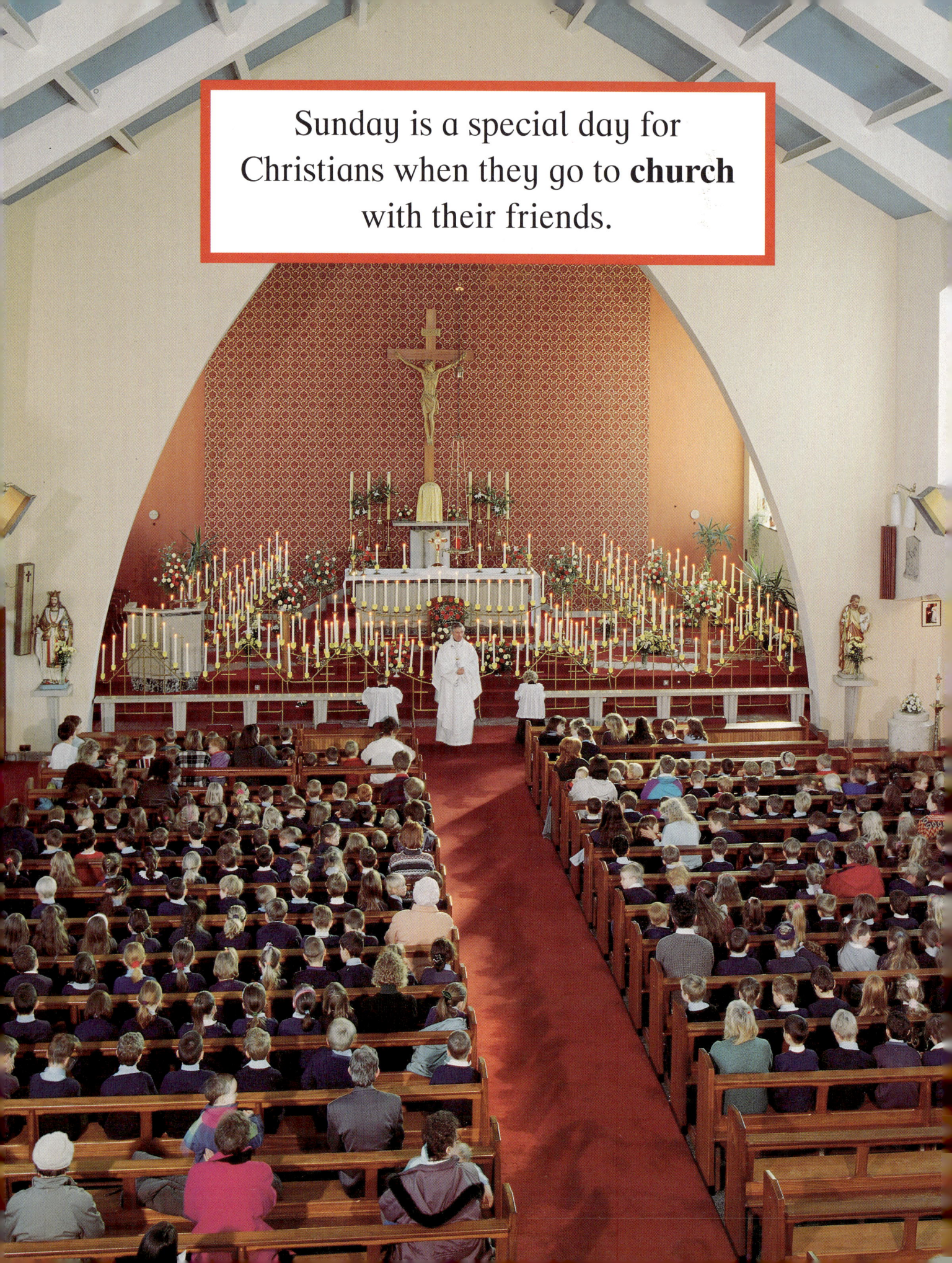

Everyone shows how much they love Jesus by singing songs about him.

The **priest** and the children tell each other stories about Jesus, just like Jesus used to tell stories to his friends.

In Sunday School, everybody is learning about how much God loves them and cares for them.

11

Jacob and Matthew are being baptized today. It is a way of saying welcome to God's family.

Some Christians wait until they are grown up before they are baptized.

Some of the older children are finding out more about being a Christian.

Daniel's sister was confirmed today. She was given a certificate to remind her of this special day when she became a member of the Church.

Lisa and her sons are saying a thank-you prayer for the meal they are going to eat together.

Sometimes we feel very unhappy or lonely. Maria finds it comforting to share her sadness with God.

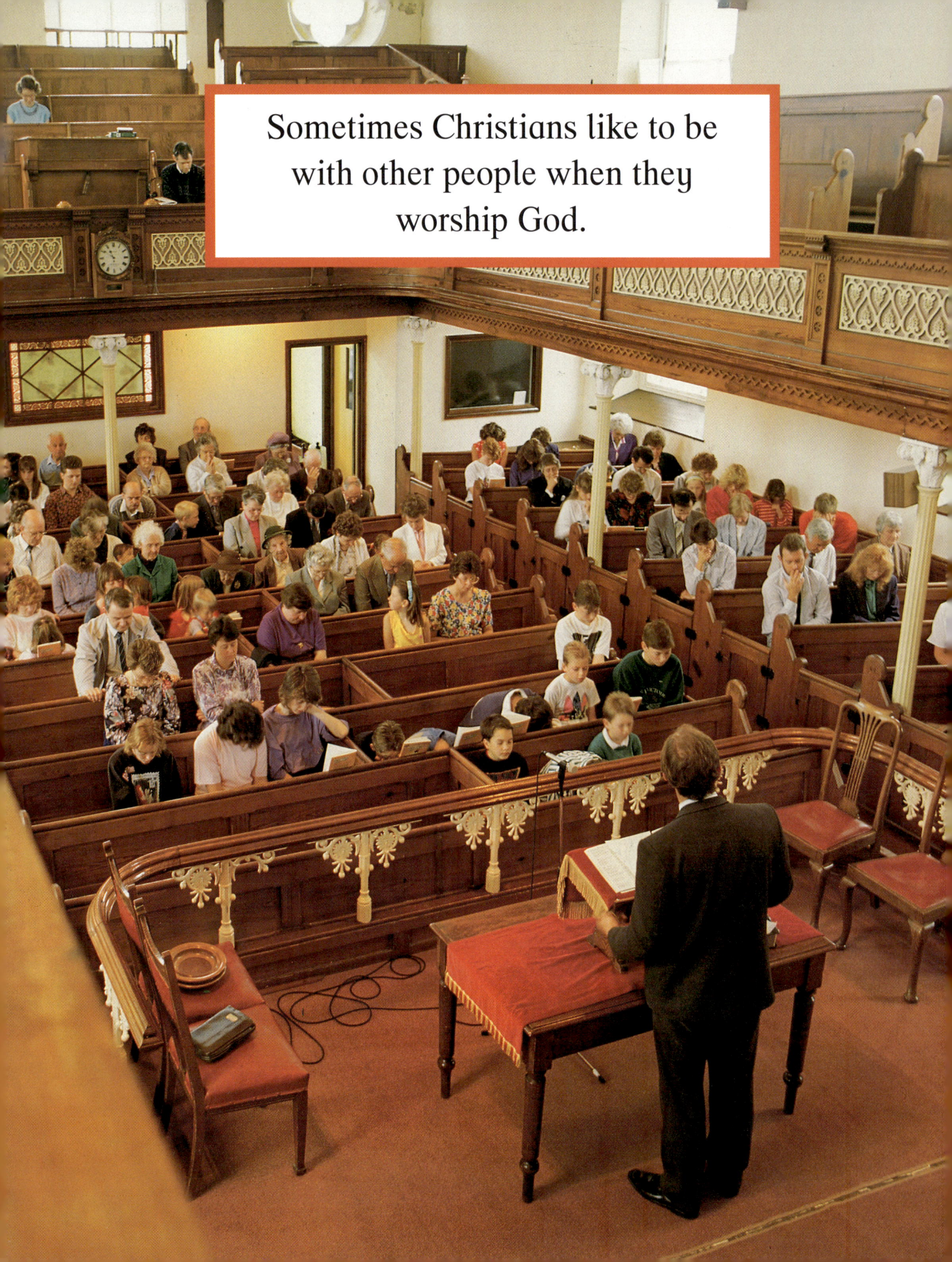

Sometimes Christians like to be with other people when they worship God.

Sometimes Christians just want to be alone to feel close to God.

It is **Palm Sunday**. Christians remember Jesus in lots of ways. David has been chosen to be Jesus, riding on a donkey.

Christians remember Jesus by having a special meal of bread and wine together.

The children have used spring flowers to make Easter decorations. They remind them of the Easter story.

Everyone has dressed up for **Easter Day**. The Easter story says 'Jesus is risen'.

Jane and Ian have invited family and friends to their wedding. It's good to share happy times together.

Last year Natalie's sister died. She has brought her friends to see her grave and talk about how they remember her.

Christians believe that Jesus is like a bright light shining in the darkness.

The Grace of our Lord Jesus Christ
and the love of God
and the fellowship of the Holy Spirit
be with us all evermore. Amen.

Notes for Teachers

Pages 4 and 5 Christians believe in God. Christian communities display considerable diversity but there are shared beliefs and teachings which bind them together. The central figure of Christianity is Jesus of Nazareth. His life, work and influence are recorded in the Gospels of Matthew, Mark, Luke and John in the part of the Bible called the New Testament.

Pages 6 and 7 There are two accounts of the birth of Jesus, one in Matthew's Gospel and one in Luke's Gospel. Christians believe that in Jesus, God became human; a way of God knowing something of the joy and the suffering all people experience in their lives.

Pages 8 and 9 Sunday is the weekly holy day for Christians when the life, death and resurrection of Jesus are commemorated. In the Christian calendar it marks the first day of a new week. Christians will usually meet together to worship, but the place is less important than the opportunity to be part of a Christian community. For many Christians worship involves music and singing of all kinds as a way of praising God.

Pages 10 and 11 Jesus used story-telling as a way of communicating his message, and the settings of his stories were appropriate for his audience at the time. For example Jesus often described God as a shepherd tending his flock. Generations of people have learned to love these stories and have come to understand their meaning with the help of Christian teachers and leaders, and through the life and example of other Christians.

Pages 12 and 13 Since the beginning of Christian history, baptism has been the accepted form of membership of the Christian community. The ceremony is often carried out during early childhood but can be undertaken at any time in life. Some Christians feel that a young child cannot understand for himself or herself the full meaning of the ritual, and so prefer to baptize adults who have come to the decision for themselves.

Pages 14 and 15 Confirmation or church membership represents the next stage after infant baptism, and gives an individual the chance to confirm the promises originally made on his or her behalf. Those who are interested in confirmation will often attend a series of classes with clergy and other Christians in which they can discuss fully the implications of being a Christian. A special service is held in church to welcome new members into the church community.

Pages 16 and 17 Christians believe they

share in God's world and praying to God, either alone or in a group, is an opportunity to say thank you for the good things in life. In times of suffering, the Christian belief that God, in Jesus, understands humanity, is both a comfort and reassurance.

Pages 18 and 19 Christians can worship anywhere from an elaborate cathedral to an open field. The early Christians met to worship in each others' homes and many still do this today. Just as there are many different types of Christians, there are many different ways of worshipping God. Sometimes an object is used as a focus of worship; a cross or crucifix, a statue, a picture, an icon or some prayer beads.

Pages 20 and 21 The stories of Jesus are told not only because they remind Christians about his life, but also because their meaning lies at the heart of the Christian faith. The events of Palm Sunday, when Jesus rode into Jerusalem on a donkey, mark the beginning of Holy Week and the Christian commemoration of the last days in the life of Jesus. The symbolic meal of bread and wine is referred to by several names: the Eucharist (thanksgiving), the Mass, the Lord's Supper or Holy Communion. It is the opportunity for Christians to re-enact the last meal that Jesus shared with his friends before his death.

Pages 22 and 23 The Gospels tell how Jesus came into conflict with the authorities in Jerusalem, was arrested, condemned to death and crucified. He rose from the dead. His tomb was discovered to be empty. He met with his followers, even sharing meals with them. Some weeks later his followers reported how they had watched Jesus being taken into heaven promising that he would return at the end of the world. The belief in the death and resurrection of Jesus is often reflected in the rituals of Easter worship; the sombre reflective mood of Good Friday contrasting with the blaze of colour, light and new life associated with Easter Day.

Pages 24 and 25 Christian marriage is seen as a serious undertaking involving not only the two partners but also their families, friends and the Christian community. The blessing of God is given on their partnership in the hope that it will be a life-long union. Some Christians see this as a divine covenant which can never be broken.

The end of life is a sombre occasion. Christians, however, believe that although death is a sad parting from earthly life, people live on in the memory of others, and through Jesus they have the promise of eternal life in the care of God.

Pages 26 and 27 The symbol of Jesus as the light of the world has always been a powerful one for Christians, rooted in many Biblical references. Candles are burned to represent God's presence in the world and some Christians also use them as an aid to prayer, believing that as the flame burns and points upwards their prayers are transported to God.

Glossary

The Bible An important book for all Christians.

Christians People who believe in God and God's son Jesus.

church A building in which Christians meet together and worship.

Easter Day The most important Christian festival, which celebrates the rising of Jesus from the dead. Christians believe Jesus brings new life for them.

Jesus Christians believe that Jesus is the son of God.

Palm Sunday The first day of Holy Week (the week before Easter) when Christians remember the last week in the life of Jesus.

priest A man or woman who performs religious ceremonies. Sometimes called a vicar, a minister or a pastor.

Further Information

Books to Read

Karyn Henley, *The Beginner's Bible*, Kingsway Publications, 1989.
Bible stories for young readers. Simple text with colourful illustrations.

Lois Rock, A First Look Series: *God, Jesus, The Church, The Bible*, Lion Publishing, 1994.
An introduction to basic Christian beliefs related to the everyday experiences of young children.

Margaret Cooling and Diane Walker, *Resource Bank Books 1, 2 & 3*, Bible Society, 1993.
Ideas and activities for celebrating Christian festivals. A practical resource book for those working with young children.

Christopher Herbert, *Prayers for Children*, The National Society, 1993.
An inspiring and imaginative collection of traditional and new prayers.

Multimedia

The Children's Video Bible Series, (1–5) Oxford Vision, available from Lion Publishers.

Eggshells and Thunderbolts, BBC Education and Culham College Institute, 1993.
A multimedia resource pack about religious education and Christianity in the primary classroom.

Song Collections

Peter Churchill, *Feeling Good*, The National Society, 1995.
A collection of songs with easy piano accompaniments and guitar chords. Many of the songs involve actions and movement.

Judy Jarvis, *Big Blue Planet*, Stainer & Bell Ltd, 1995.
A collection of more than eighty songs reflecting children's experiences of daily life.

Index

baptism 12, 13
Bible 5, 30

Christians 4, 6, 7, 13, 14, 18, 19, 21, 26, 30
Christmas 6
church 8, 30
confirmation 15

death 25

Easter 22, 23, 30

family 4, 24
friends 8, 10, 24, 25

God 7, 11, 12, 17, 18, 19, 27

Jesus 5, 6, 7, 9, 10, 20, 21, 23, 26, 27, 30
Palm Sunday 20, 30
prayer 16, 27

priest 10, 30

singing 9
stories 5, 10, 23
Sunday 8
Sunday school 11

wedding 24
worship 8, 18